This book belongs to:

_____

_____

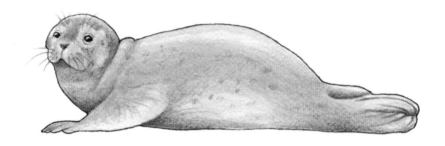

CURIOUS KIDS NATURE GUIDE

Curious Kids
NATURE GUIDE

Explore the Amazing Outdoors
of the **PACIFIC NORTHWEST**

FIONA COHEN
Illustrated by **MARNI FYLLING**

little bigfoot
an imprint of sasquatch books
seattle, wa

Manufactured in China by C&C Offset Printing Co. Ltd.
Shenzhen, Guangdong Province, in December 2016

Published by Little Bigfoot, an imprint of Sasquatch Books
21 20 19 18 17   9 8 7 6 5 4 3 2 1

Editors: Tegan Tigani, Christy Cox
Production editor: Emma Reh
Cover design: Anna Goldstein
Interior design: Bryce de Flamand
Copyeditor: Janice Lee

Library of Congress Cataloging-in-Publication Data
is available.

ISBN: 978-1-63217-083-5

Sasquatch Books
1904 Third Avenue, Suite 710
Seattle, WA 98101
(206) 467-4300
www.sasquatchbooks.com
custserv@sasquatchbooks.com

CONTENTS

INTRODUCTION

This is a book about where the Pacific Ocean meets the northwest coast of North America. It's a place with soaring mountains, giant trees, glow-in-the-dark seawater, and stupendous slugs.

This area is called the Pacific Northwest, or Cascadia, and includes Washington, Oregon, and the Alaska Panhandle in the United States, and British Columbia in Canada.

Whatever you call it, if you're lucky enough to live there or visit it, there's a lot of spectacular nature to discover. Whether you're in the woods, at the beach, by a stream or a swamp, or in your own backyard, there's plenty to find.

So go outside and discover what's there. This book will help you begin.

Here's what you'll need to do to get started:

1. Use your senses. The more you stay still and quiet and examine what is around you, the more you'll find. Amazing animals could be nearby, but if you don't take the time to wait and watch, you might never find them. Listen, smell, and touch as you go.

2. Stay comfortable. It's hard to enjoy nature and discover new things when your feet hurt; you're cold, hungry, or thirsty; or you're worried about sliming your best outfit. Wear comfortable shoes and sturdy clothes. Dress for the weather, whether it's hot, cold, rainy, or all three. Be ready to change your clothing with the weather. If you're going on a longer hike, bring food, water, and a first aid kit.

3. Take care of nature. When you're done exploring, leave everything as you found it.

- Put back rocks and logs you moved. Animals rely on them for shelter.

- Pick up litter, even if it isn't yours.

- Collecting a few leaves, sticks, rocks, or shells is fine, but leave living things where they are.

- Don't feed wildlife.

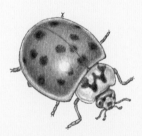

- Don't break plants.

- Obey the rules of the trail.

4. Stay safe.

- Don't go out alone. It's fun to explore with a friend, a sibling, or an adult.

- If you go on an expedition, get permission and share your plans with a responsible adult. Let him or her know exactly where you are going.

Let's explore!

FOREST

When you're exploring the forest, it's important to look and listen all around.

Above your head, many animals and plants live among the upper branches of trees. Some never come down. By your feet is an intricate world of creatures that live their lives among the decaying twigs, leaves, and needles.

Some of the biggest living things in the world grow here, but so do some of the smallest. Insects, mites, and microscopic bacteria are all part of the forest ecosystem.

DOUGLAS FIR | *Pseudotsuga menziesii (left)*
WESTERN RED CEDAR | *Thuja plicata (right)*

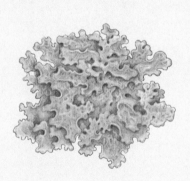

LUNGWORT
Lobaria pulmonaria

LICORICE FERN
Polypodium glycyrrhiza

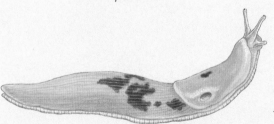

BANANA SLUG
Ariolimax columbianus

BLACK-TAILED DEER
Odocoileus hemionus columbianus

PACIFIC TRILLIUM
Trillium ovatum

DOUGLAS SQUIRREL
Tamiasciurus douglasii

QUESTIONABLE STROPHARIA
Stropharia ambigua (left)

CORAL MUSHROOM
Clavulina (right)

ROUGH-SKINNED NEWT
Taricha granulosa

BARRED OWL
Strix varia

GREAT HORNED OWL
Bubo virginianus

RED-BREASTED
NUTHATCH
Sitta canadensis

WESTERN SCREECH OWL
Megascops kennicottii

BROWN CREEPER
Certhia americana

BLACK-CAPPED
CHICKADEE
Poecile atricapillus

PILEATED WOODPECKER
Dryocopus pileatus

RAVEN
Corvus corax

PACIFIC DAMPWOOD TERMITE
Zootermopsis angusticollis

YELLOW-SPOTTED MILLIPEDE
Harpaphe haydeniana

WESTERN THATCHING ANT
Formica obscuripes

BANANA SLUGS are the second-biggest slugs in the world. They can be black, brown, yellow, or white with spots. (The yellow ones with spots look a lot like little old bananas.) They can grow up to ten inches long. They glide around the forest floor from Southeast Alaska to Northern California, munching on fruits and leaves and gobbling up mushrooms.

Everything banana slugs do involves slime. They use slime to keep from drying out and to protect them from sharp edges; they can glide over broken glass or razor blades without getting a nick. They also use slime to ward off snakes, shrews, and salamanders that try to eat them. Often the would-be slug-snacker ends up gagging on a mouthful of mucus. Sometimes slugs use slime to send messages. A slug can find a mate by following its slime trail.

Slugs are *hermaphrodites*. This means they are male and female at the same time. Once a slug finds a mate, the two climb a tree together and then dangle off a branch, hanging from a rope of slime.

If you step on a slug barefoot, you'll get a toe-load of clammy, sticky goo. If you try to use water to clean it off, the goo will only swell. The way to get it off is to rub, and keep rubbing.

ROUGH-SKINNED NEWTS roam the moss in damp corners of the forest. When they feel threatened, they arch their backs to flash their bright-orange bellies. The belly is a warning—a newt's bumpy skin has enough poison in it to kill a person if eaten. (If you ever touch one, wash your hands.) Some garter snakes have a resistance to the poison and can eat the newts. But sometimes a garter snake will try to eat a newt and give up, concluding it is too poisonous.

Most OWLS are nocturnal, which means they are active and hunt at night, but sometimes you can spot them in the daytime. One way to try to find them is to use your ears. If a crow or a jay finds an owl, it will make loud calls until all the other crows and jays in the area surround the owl. They'll keep calling at it, and the boldest ones will swoop at it. If you hear a bunch of birds making a ruckus in the trees, look at what they are up to.

Owls have good eyes and very keen ears. One ear is higher than the other, which helps the owl pinpoint exactly where a sound is coming from. Owls are also quiet fliers. Their flight feathers have special edges that muffle sound. A mouse on the ground won't hear the owl coming until it is too late.

Owls eat small animals, such as mice, shrews, and squirrels. When they catch their prey, they don't spend a lot of time taking it apart. Instead, they swallow it whole or in large chunks. Later on, they'll vomit up a pellet of bones and hair and other bits they couldn't digest. They most often do this at the tree where they roost.

If you see an owl in a tree, take a look around the base. If there's a lot of bird poop there, the owl likely goes there a lot and you have a good chance of finding a pellet. If you find one of those pellets and take it apart, you can figure out what the owl ate. Sometimes, if you are careful, you can put together an entire tiny skeleton.

You can find different kinds of owls in different places. In the forest you most often find barred, great horned, and western screech owls.

RAVENS look like crows, but they can weigh more than twice as much. The raven is one of the most intelligent and playful birds in the world. Sometimes they will fly upside down, somersault in the air, or slide on snow.

They eat what they can find: eggs and chicks of other birds, dead animals, and insects. They like to soar high in the air, which is a good way to spot a dead animal lying on the ground.

When they call out to other ravens, their deep voices can carry a mile or more. Scientists have classified more than thirty kinds of raven calls. These smart birds have a lot to say.

CHICKADEES are the leaders of the winter flocks, which move from tree to tree, eating bugs and other tidbits, and chirping to each other. They often call by repeating their name: "chickadee-dee-dee." "Chicka-dee-dee-dee" can mean a variety of things. Sometimes they call "chickadee-dee" to scold an intruder. Other times they call "chickadee-dee" to let each other know where they are. They fly from tree to tree, hopping around in the branches and bark to look for seeds and bugs. Chickadees can eat upside down, which comes in handy when dinner is dangling at the end of a twig.

RED-BREASTED NUTHATCHES and **BROWN CREEPERS** search for insects on the trunks and large branches of trees. Creepers start at the bottom of trees and walk right side up. Nuthatches start at the top and walk upside down. Scientists aren't sure why nuthatches go down trees headfirst, but it may be that, from that angle, they can find bugs that the creepers miss.

WOODPECKERS pound on trees for three reasons. One reason is to communicate. In the spring they drum on trees to find mates and to claim a piece of the forest as their own. Another reason is to feed, catching ants, beetles, and termites living in the tree. Many woodpeckers have tongues that are longer than their heads. They can stick their tongues into cracks in wood and grab bugs.

Woodpecker's tongues are different depending on the species. The pileated woodpecker's tongue is hooked at the end and coated with sticky spit. When woodpeckers aren't feeding, their tongues coil back into their heads, around their brains.

A pileated woodpecker's tongue fits far inside its head.

The third reason woodpeckers pound on trees is to build a home. Male and female woodpeckers will work together for over

To hit a tree as hard as a woodpecker does, you'd have to run toward it as fast as you can and smack your face into it, again and again, more than a thousand times a minute.

It would hurt, right? Not if you were a woodpecker. They have thick skulls, and they clench some of the muscles of their faces to absorb the shock. Feathers over their nostrils keep them from breathing in the splinters. Extra eyelids keep their eyeballs from popping out of their heads.

two weeks to peck out a nest in a tree, creating a tunnel with a large hollow inside. They line the hollowed-out area with leftover wood chips.

Woodpeckers will almost always use a nest hole for only one year. After that, other animals move in. Some of the creatures you can find in old woodpecker holes are owls, chickadees, swallows, bats, wasps, wood ducks, flying squirrels, and pine martens.

DOUGLAS SQUIRRELS are noisy. They chatter at each other and at other animals, even people. They feast on the seeds in Douglas fir cones. The squirrels run up the tree and bite the cones off so they will fall to the ground. If you walk under the tree when that is happening, a cone might land on your head.

Fir cones are covered with scales, each of which has a seed tucked inside. Douglas squirrels pick off the scales one by one, eating the seeds, and leave a pile of scales behind. They also hide some cones away for later.

The squirrels don't usually need to eat all the seeds they hide, which is good for the tree. Left alone, some of these hidden seeds will break open, and a young plant will start to grow, sending out its first root and a stem with a crown of delicate needles, forming a seedling.

Most deer in the Pacific Northwest are **BLACK-TAILED DEER**. They like to be at the edge of the forest—in woods near meadows or in meadows near woods. In many Pacific Northwest cities and towns, people find deer strolling through neighborhoods and stopping to eat the roses.

In late spring and summer mother deer (does) give birth to their babies (fawns). The fawns have spotted fur that blends in with the forest floor, so would-be predators have a hard time noticing them amid the spotted patterns of light filtering through leaves. For the first few weeks of their lives, fawns spend most of their time lying still. During this time, does clean their fawns, eat their feces, and drink their urine to make sure their odor doesn't attract predators.

Does aren't as good as fawns at staying hidden or camouflaged, so they stay away from their fawns for hours at a time but return every so often to feed and clean them. If you find a fawn alone in the woods, don't worry. Its mother will return to take care of it.

What's black and yellow and smells like almonds? The **YELLOW-SPOTTED MILLIPEDE**. If a predator attacks, the millipede will roll into a ball, and a poisonous cyanide gas will come out of tiny holes in its sides. It won't hurt you, but if you do pick one up, you should wash your hands before eating.

Yellow-spotted millipedes chew through needles and leaves on the forest floor. Though the prefix *milli* means thousand and *pede* means foot or feet, millipedes don't have a thousand feet. Male yellow-spotted millipedes have sixty feet, and females have sixty-two.

Near sunset on evenings in late summer, hundreds of **PACIFIC DAMPWOOD TERMITES**, brownish insects that some people call flying ants, crawl out of dead trees and take flight, searching for mates and places to build new colonies.

A male and female pair find a log that is just rotten enough and become parents to a colony of soldiers and workers, who chew through wood and live in the tunnels they create. Bacteria in their guts make it possible for them to digest the wood. Once a year, a few of the workers and soldiers grow long wings, turn from white to amber, and develop sex organs, and take flight in search of mates.

WESTERN THATCHING ANTS live in domes built out of twigs, leaves, and needles. The biggest ones can be two or even three feet high. The nests are home to a colony of thousands of ants, and there's more to the nests than you can see. They include networks of tunnels that can reach four feet under the mounds. Some scientists think that the mounds help the ants keep the colonies cool in the summer and warm in the winter.

Western Thatching Ant Nest

You can see many sizes of ants scrambling in and out of the entrances to the nest. They are all workers, though they tend to take different roles in the colony. Some have indoor jobs, such as looking after the mother ants, or queens, and their eggs and wormlike babies, called larvae, deep in the mound. Western thatching ants can have dozens of queens in a single mound.

These two western thatching ants are different sizes, but they are both workers from the same colony.

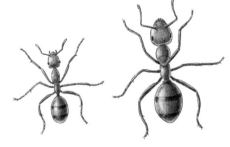

Some worker ants spend more time outside, building up the outside of the nest or finding food. Looking around the nest, you can see places where the ants have cleared out paths along the ground: clear spaces with a steady stream of ants going back and forth.

Western thatching ants eat plants, insects, and spiders. They also get food from small insects called aphids, which eat plant sap. When an ant strokes an aphid a particular way, the aphid will ooze a drop of liquid. This aphid goo, called honeydew, is sugary and delicious to ants. In exchange for the honeydew the ants protect the aphids. They might move the aphids around to better spots on plants or put them in a sheltered spot during bad weather. Scientists call this kind of cooperation between species *mutualism*.

Ants cooperate in everything, even eating. When a foraging western thatching ant eats, it stores some of the food in a special stomach. A hungry ant can go up to a full ant and touch a special spot by the ant's mouth to cause the full ant to vomit a meal into the hungry ant's mouth. It's like pushing the button on a water fountain. Scientists call it *trophallaxis*. It looks like the ants are kissing.

TRILLIUM, a wildflower, relies on ants to move its seeds around on the forest floor. The seeds have oily parts that ants love to eat. Ants gather the seeds and bring them back to their colonies.

When they've eaten the oily parts, they pick up what is left of the seed and drop it in an ant garbage dump. In another spring the ant garbage dump will sprout a new clump of trillium.

Douglas Fir (left), Western Red Cedar (right)

DOUGLAS FIRS have very thick, rough bark. You might find an old Douglas fir that has blackened bark, the only sign left that there was a fire in that forest a long time ago. The fire burned the ferns and shrubs all around this tree, but the tree survived.

Some of the biggest trees in the world grow in Pacific Northwest forests. Why do big trees thrive here? It's because of the weather. During the wet winters they store water in their trunks. In the summer it is often dry, and it is hard for smaller plants to survive, but trees can keep growing using their stored-up water.

A SIMPLE WAY TO FIGURE OUT THE HEIGHT OF A TREE

You need to be on level ground and have a long tape measure. First, find a straight stick that is as long as your arm. Then stand back from the tree, holding the stick out upright, with the bottom of the stick at eye level. Walk to a place where the bottom of the stick lines up with the bottom of the tree, and the top of the stick lines up with the top of the tree. You are now as far away from the tree as the tree is tall. Measure the distance to the tree, and, give or take a few bumps in the ground, you have the tree's height.

WESTERN RED CEDARS have gray-brown stringy bark. You might see an old cedar tree missing a strip of bark from its trunk. The bare spot will be at its widest at the bottom and taper to a point high above your head. That bare area may be a spot where Native Americans carefully peeled the bark away from the tree to make all kinds of things, including ropes, baskets, capes, and hats.

Stumps or logs that lie in the forest long enough might become **NURSE LOGS**. An old log with a layer of leaves and needles on top makes a nice space for a seedling to grow. As the young plant grows, insects, fungi, and other living things will turn the log into soil for the new trees. Someday the only sign of that log ever being there will be a group of trees all growing in a straight line.

Plants, lichens, fungi, and other living things that grow on living plants are called *epiphytes*. You can find epiphytes on all tree species in Pacific Northwest forests, but one species has the most epiphytes of all: the big-leaf maple. These trees have huge pillows of epiphytes so old and thick that over the years they start to form their own soil on the tree branches and trunk where they grow. This soil is so thick that big-leaf maples grow roots from their branches, taking in water and nutrients far above the ground.

LICORICE FERN is an epiphyte that grows on rocks and tree branches, especially on big-leaf maples. Its leaves and stems die in the summer, when the soil on the maple branches is dry. When the rains come in the fall, the fern grows back again. Its *rhizomes*, the part of it that is under the soil, taste like licorice.

LUNGWORT grows on tree branches and is another example of an epiphyte. It's a lichen, a combination of a fungus and one or two other life forms. (In the case of lungwort, it's a fungus, an alga, and a bacterium.) Lungwort grows on tree branches. It is able to do something most trees can't do: get nitrogen from the air. When the lungwort falls to the ground, it fertilizes the soil, and the tree can get the nitrogen it needs to grow.

You can find many other kinds of lichen in the forest. They can look like leaves, rags, sticks, nets, cups, strings, scales, and even pimples. Some look like crusts, and some look like hair.

They grow in a variety of colors, such as gray, white, black, green, brown, orange, and even bright yellow.

MUSHROOMS pop up from the forest floor and spring from rotten logs. Different species show up at different times of year, but if you want to see a lot of mushrooms, the best time to look is a few days after the first big rains of fall. Mushrooms are the most visible part of a fungus, which otherwise grows out of sight all year long. A fungus grows as a network of tiny tubes called *hyphae*, often underground or running through a rotten log, a living plant or animal, or even another fungus. Some of these tiny tubes are so small that you can only see them with a microscope.

Mushrooms are the parts of fungi that carry spores. If you shake a mushroom over your hand, you can see the spores. They look like fine dust, and there are many thousands of them. Some mushrooms, such as the artist's conk, have billions. Each spore is much tinier and simpler than a plant's seed but still has the capability to become a new fungus.

Mushrooms don't have to be mushroom shaped. They can look like corals, cauliflower, blobs of jelly, cups, or shelves. A few of them glow in the dark.

Some fungi help decompose, or break down, dead plants and animals. Others are parasites—they push their tiny tubes into living plants, animals, or even other fungi, eating them from the inside out.

BEACH

The moon and the sun pull on the earth's oceans to make tides. Storms and currents rearrange beaches and even wear down rocks. And the many things that live on the shore also leave a mark.

When you explore a beach, come ready to get wet. Some of the most amazing creatures live in tide pools or damp spots, or at the water's edge. It helps to bring a bucket or two, so you can take a closer look at things you find.

Turn over rocks to see what is underneath, but be gentle. Put everything back the way you find it. If you go out at low tide, keep an eye on the water: what is part of the beach at low tide could turn into an island as the water returns.

TIDEPOOL SCULPIN
Oligocottus maculosus

PURPLE SHORE CRAB
Hemigrapsus nudus

NORTHERN CLINGFISH
Gobiesox maeandricus

MASK LIMPET
Tectura persona

BLUEBAND HERMIT CRAB
Pagurus samuelis

**NORTHERN
BAY MUSSEL**
Mytilus trossulus

ECCENTRIC SAND DOLLAR
Dendraster excentricus

**GOOSENECK
BARNACLE**
Pollicipes polymerus

ACORN BARNACLE
Balanus glandula

COMMON PERIWINKLE
Littorina littorea

RED TUBE WORM
Serpula vermicularis

LITTLENECK CLAM
Protothaca staminea

AGGREGATING ANEMONES
Anthopleura elegantissima

PURPLE SEA URCHIN
Strongylocentrotus purpuratus

MOSSY CHITON
Mopalia muscosa

LEWIS'S MOON SNAIL
Euspira lewisii

MOON JELLY
Aurelia labiata

PURPLE SEA STAR
Pisaster ochraceus

GREAT BLUE HERON
Ardea Herodias

GULL
Larus

BRANT
Branta bernicla

BUFFLEHEAD
Bucephala albeola

WESTERN GREBE
*Aechmophorus
occidentalis*

HARLEQUIN DUCK
Histrionicus histrionicus

OSPREY
Pandion haliaetus

BALD EAGLE
*Haliaeetus
leucocephalus*

ROCKWEED
Fucus distichus

HARBOR SEAL
Phoca vitulina

STELLER SEA LION
Eumetopias jubatus

SEA OTTER
Enhydra lutris

**NORTH AMERICAN
RIVER OTTER**
Lontra canadensis

ORCA
Orcinus orca

BULL KELP
Nereocystis luetkeana

The water is full of living things called **PLANKTON**. Most of them are too small to see on their own, but when a lot of them are there, the water becomes blue green and cloudy.

Most animals in the sea, from shrimp to blue whales, depend on this soup of plants and tiny animals. They eat plankton, or they eat creatures that eat plankton. And for part of their lives, many creatures, including starfish, clams, and crabs, *are* plankton.

If you go out on a moonless summer night and stir up some water, you might see pale glowing sparks. These are a type of plankton called *dinoflagellates*—one-celled life-forms that, under the microscope, look like eggs with tails attached. Some scientists think that dinoflagellates glow when something, such as a small fish, is trying to eat them. Bigger fish notice the glow and eat the small fish, while the dinoflagellate escapes.

TIDEPOOL SCULPINS are fish with spots and stripes that help them blend in with the rocks. When the tide comes in, they forage beyond their pools, but when the tide goes out, each sculpin likes to return to its own pool.

The **NORTHERN CLINGFISH** hangs on to the underside of rocks using a big suction cup on its belly. The suction cup is strong, so strong it can lift more than three hundred times the fish's weight. It helps the fish hang on in rough water and also enables it to eat limpets. Northern clingfish live and lay eggs in their damp hiding places on the beach. To get by when the tide goes out, they have another talent: they can breathe air if they need to.

When the tide goes out, **SHORE CRABS** wriggle into the damp places under rocks. These crabs breathe through gills, like a fish, so they need to stay wet.

Pick a rock up on the beach and you might see a crowd of tiny crabs scuttling out of the way. Most of them are likely too small to pinch you. If a crab is big enough to pinch you, gently pick it up by holding it behind the pincers on the sides of the big shell covering the main part of its body. With your fingers there, the crab can wave its claws at you, but it can't reach you.

Crabs, like insects and spiders, have bodies covered in shells, which are also called *exoskeletons*. As a crab grows, it gets too big for its exoskeleton, so it grows a new one underneath, and when this new shell

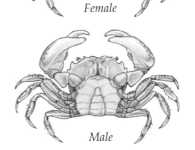

Female

Male

is ready, the crab breaks out of the old one and leaves it on the beach. A lot of crab shells you find on the beach are shells that were left behind when the crab got bigger.

You can tell if a crab is male or female by looking at its belly. If it is female, the plates of its exoskeleton will be in the shape of a half oval, which looks like a beehive. Sometimes there are eggs tucked inside the oval. If it is male, the plates will form a shape that looks like a lighthouse—a tower with a thin bit on top.

If you look a **HERMIT CRAB** in the face, it looks tough. It has huge claws and a hard exoskeleton over its body. But the armor goes only so far. Hermit crabs' abdomens are soft, so they need to keep them in shells. The abdomen curls and grips the shell with the help of two little flipper-like tabs called *uropods*.

If something threatens the crab, it can retreat into the shell, blocking the opening with its big left claw. Leave it be and wait a while, and it will bring its legs, eyes, and antennae out again.

The shell won't take care of the hermit crab forever. Eventually, the crab will grow too large for its shell and will need a bigger one. It may also switch shells if it finds one it likes better. The trouble is, if another hermit crab likes it too, they have to wrestle for it.

MUSSELS are bivalve mollusks. *Bivalve* means they have two shells. They attach themselves to rocks by making several hundred threads of special glue. The glue is stretchy, so the mussel can move back and forth with the ocean's waves, but at the same time it's stronger than the steel people use to construct buildings. A mussel underwater can squirt out a strand of this glue within five minutes. As soon as it touches the rock, shell, or boat it's aimed at, it will stick.

LIMPETS are mollusks too, but they are *gastropods*, which means that the biggest part of their body is a muscular foot. (Slugs and snails are also gastropods.) A limpet's foot can cling to a rock so tightly that if you tug on it, you are more likely to break the limpet's shell than loosen the foot's grip on the rock.

BARNACLES lead a simple life. They reside inside crusty shells, with their heads glued to rocks. When the tide comes in, they open a door at the top of their shells, stretch out their legs, or *cirri*, and use them to grab tiny living things that float in the water.

But that isn't the whole story. Each barnacle starts life inside its mother's shell, where it stays until it grows into a creature called a *nauplius*, which is smaller than the period at the end of this sentence. It has a shell, one eye, and six legs, and emerges from its mother's shell to swim around with thousands of other *nauplii* (the plural of nauplius) in the plankton.

Some of the nauplii get swept into the mouths of their own parents. Other predators gobble up many of the rest. Those that survive grow into *cyprids*, with three eyes, two shells, and twelve legs.

Cyprids can swim well, but they can't eat. Once a barnacle becomes a cyprid it lives on fat reserves until it can glue its head to its very own rock. Then it starts building a six-plated shell.

Barnacles are hermaphrodites. They can all lay eggs and all have penises—extra-long penises that can be up to eight times their body length. Because their heads are cemented to rocks, their penises must be long enough to reach outside of their shells and into their neighbors' shells, where the eggs are.

The kind of barnacles you might find depends on where they are on the beach. Near the high-tide mark, where there are few opportunities for plankton meals, the barnacles are tiny. Lower down the beach they get bigger and denser, carpeting the rocks in gray, until you get low enough, and then they disappear. The reason is, with a low enough tide, the beach becomes a good environment for snails that eat barnacles.

On beaches with lots of waves, you find **GOOSENECK BARNACLES**. The shells of these are at the end of flexible, leathery necks, which move with the waves so the barnacles can hang on more tightly.

SAND DOLLARS live low on the beach and are covered in water most of the time. They eat plankton and a lot of sand. Most of the sand goes right through their bodies, but the sand dollars store some heavy sand grains inside their bodies as a kind of weight belt so that water currents don't sweep them away. Sand dollar shells are beautiful, and it's fine to collect the bleached hollow remains of the animal. But if it is covered in tiny spines, it's still alive, and it should be left alone.

The **CLAM**, like the mussel, is a bivalve mollusk, and it digs into the sand using its muscular foot. It has a long stretchy siphon that goes up through the hole to the top of the sand. The siphon draws in seawater and lets it out. Clams eat by filtering seawater for plankton.

If you're walking on the beach at low tide, you can see the siphons as little holes in the sand. Poke your finger in the hole, or stomp on the sand next to it, and the clam will draw its siphon back below the sand, letting off a spurt of water.

The **GEODUCK** (pronounced "gooey duck") is the biggest clam on the beach and can live for more than 150 years. It can weigh up to eight pounds, and its body is too big to fit into its shell. A geoduck can dig four feet under the mud, with its siphon stretched way up to the surface to bring in seawater. If a predator tries to grab the siphon, the geoduck pulls it down. If the predator manages to grab the siphon before it disappears, that doesn't mean the geoduck is caught. The siphon breaks off and the big clam stays out of reach.

PERIWINKLES are tiny snails that live in the highest parts of the beach. They don't need to be in the water much. When one is high and dry, it closes a door, called an *operculum*, over its body and makes glue to stay stuck on the rock. Periwinkles are so tough that if you feed one to a sea anemone, it will come out unharmed and with a shinier shell.

AGGREGATING ANEMONES live attached to rocks. At low tide you can find patches of them carpeting rocks. They can have babies by sending eggs and sperm into the water, or they can clone themselves by splitting in two.

When you see a carpet of anemones on a rock, they're probably a group of clones of each other. If an anemone that is not from their clone group settles near them, the aggregating anemones will sting the outsider with their tentacles. Sometimes you can see two clone groups on a rock. On one side there is a carpet of one clone, and on the other side there is a carpet of another. Between the two carpets is a thin line where no anemone can settle without getting stung on both sides.

The farther down the beach you go, the more kinds of creatures you can find. Most of the time, the bottom of the beach is underwater. Every rock there is covered with living things. A lot of the plants and animals on the beach are covered in living things too. Make sure you look in every pool and crevice, and check under rocks and blades of seaweed.

These anemones are green because they have plants called *algae* living inside them. The algae are so small that they can only be seen through a microscope. They live inside the anemone and give it energy from the sun. When anemones settle in the shade, the algae plants can't live, so they turn white.

TUBE WORMS look like downy feathers in the water. But touch them and they'll spring their tentacles back into their tubular shells. These animals are distant relatives of earthworms.

The **MOSSY CHITON** hangs on to rocks and blends into them. You can find the mossy chiton on the middle and lower parts of the beach. Eight interlocking shells cover its back and the tough brown skin around the shells is covered in hairs that look like seaweed. The hairs have sensitive nerve fibers in them.

The **PURPLE SEA URCHIN** can rub at a rock with its teeth and spines until it has hollowed out its own hideout. Sea urchins move around on tube feet. Their feet are long so that they can reach past their inch-long spines. If you find sea urchins on a beach, it means that the water is fairly clean. Sea urchins are some of the first creatures to die off when water becomes polluted.

A **MOON SNAIL**'s shell can grow to be the size of an apple, but its foot can grow to be the size of a loaf of bread. The snail can puff up its foot by sucking seawater into its body. It can also squeeze the water out of its foot and tuck the foot back in its shell if it has to.

The moon snail's big foot is helpful when it is tunneling under the sand in search of clams to eat. When it catches a clam, it wraps its foot around it. Then it uses its toothed tongue to scrape a neat round hole in the clam's shell, sticks its mouth and tongue through the hole, and eats every soft bit of the clam. When you find clamshells on the beach with round holes punched in them, you know a moon snail ate the clams.

Another sign of moon snails is a sand collar. It looks like a circle of rubber mixed with sand. The female makes them as cases for her eggs. First she covers her foot with a layer of sand mixed with mucus, then she lays eggs and makes another layer of mucus mixed with sand on the other side of the eggs so that her eggs are inside a sand-and-mucus sandwich. Finally, she tunnels out of the ring, leaving behind a sand collar.

A beach predator more ferocious than the moon snail is the sun-flower sea star. It has twenty-four arms, and the touch of an oncom-ing sunflower sea star sends normally still creatures scurry-ing out of its way. For example, cockles, like other clams, spend their lives wedged into the sand, feeding on plankton, but when a sunflower sea star lays a tube foot on one, it springs into action. The cockle yanks its foot onto the surface of the sand and hops like a pole-vaulter to get out of the way.

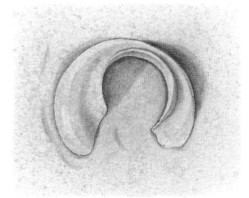

Moon snails lay their eggs in sand collars made of mucus and sand.

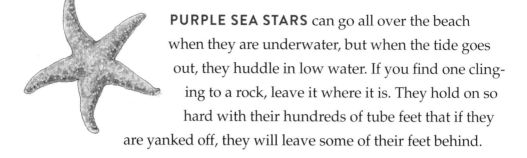

PURPLE SEA STARS can go all over the beach when they are underwater, but when the tide goes out, they huddle in low water. If you find one clinging to a rock, leave it where it is. They hold on so hard with their hundreds of tube feet that if they are yanked off, they will leave some of their feet behind.

JELLIES (often called jellyfish) float around and eat the plankton. They use long tentacles covered in stinging cells to grab tiny animals and pull them into their mouths. Where there's a lot of plankton, there will be a lot of jellies.

GREAT BLUE HERONS are impressive. An adult stands three feet tall—four feet tall with the neck stretched out—and has a six-foot wingspan and a croak like someone trying to play the saxophone for the first time. It wanders the shore eating crabs, fish, and other animals. You can often see them standing in the water, staring until they strike to catch a fish. Great blue herons nest in trees and band together in loud, smelly groups. Some of the colonies have more than five hundred nests.

GULLS, like people, are omnivores. They'll eat garbage or grains, chips or clams, french fries or fresh fish. When they catch a clam, they fly with it over hard rocks and then drop it so that the shell breaks. Sometimes you can find the rocks they use. They're the ones covered with smashed clamshells.

Gulls will steal fish that other birds catch. If you're having a picnic at the beach, they might even steal food right off your plate. They also venture into cities in search of food. You can sometimes see them in city parks picking earthworms from the lawn after a good rain.

There are several kinds of gulls in the Pacific Northwest. Most adult gulls are white with gray wings. Juvenile gulls are usually speckled grayish brown and are often as large as the adults. Sometimes you can see juveniles chasing after adults, begging for food.

BRANTS are small geese with an appetite for eelgrass, a plant that grows on sandy and muddy beaches. Some spend the winter on the Pacific Coast of the United States and Canada, while others go farther south—as far as Mexico—and stop on northwest beaches in spring as they make their way north. They have to eat a lot while they're here. They arrive in the Arctic in May and make their nests while there is still snow on the ground, so they don't get anything to eat for weeks.

WESTERN GREBES hang out in large crowds offshore. They hardly ever fly. Instead, if they feel threatened, they dive. They are wonderful divers and are good at chasing fish underwater and spearing them with their long sharp beaks. In the spring they go to inland ponds and lakes, build nests, and breed.

BUFFLEHEADS are the smallest diving ducks in North America, and some of the most punctual. They breed in sheltered forest lakes in Canada and Alaska, and return to Pacific Coast bays and lakes within the same few days every year. One town, Sidney, British Columbia, has its own holiday for the birds on the day they usually show up in town: October 15, All Buffleheads Day.

By the end of winter, after diving for fish and shrimp in local waters, the buffleheads aren't as little as they were before they arrived. Males can gain 20 percent more weight over the winter.

HARLEQUIN DUCKS like moving water. In the spring and summer they raise their families on rushing streams in the mountains. In the winter they're often coasting the waves on rocky shores.

BALD EAGLES eat fish, but they don't necessarily catch them. Often they will wait for another bird, such as a heron or a cormorant, to catch a meal, and then they will swoop down and snatch it. As eagles get older they are more likely to catch their own meals, but they won't hesitate to steal another bird's. Eagles like to build nests in tall trees near lakes, rivers, or beaches. They build the biggest nests of any bird in North America.

OSPREYS are great at catching their own fish. They hover over the water, watching, and then drop, talons out, splashing into the water to grab the fish. Their feet have pads covered in tiny hooks to help them grab their slippery prey.

Not surprisingly, they don't like bald eagles in their territories and will challenge them and chase them away, even though bald eagles are bigger. Ospreys migrate south for the winter, going as far as South America.

HARBOR SEALS are nimble swimmers. They can hold their breath for almost half an hour and snatch fish with their mouths. On land, movement is tougher as they wiggle their blubbery bodies onto the rocks. If you're lucky enough to see a seal on land, don't disturb it. It needs to rest. If you see a baby seal on land, leave it alone. Its mother is off fishing and will come back to feed her young—provided you stay away.

STELLER SEA LIONS are bigger than harbor seals, and instead of gray, they are a deep brown. They are quick swimmers, sometimes surfing in the waves or leaping like dolphins. They also like to hang out together in large groups on rocks or floating in a sheltered bay. They bark a lot. California sea lions are smaller than Steller sea lions and just as playful.

You can sometimes see **RIVER OTTERS** walking along the beach or swimming along the shoreline. You can also find them in rivers and lakes. Sometimes you might see a mother otter swimming with her babies, which are called kits. (Look for one large head and two or more smaller heads.) They leave distinctive trails in the sand—two lines of webbed footprints with scuff marks in between where the tail dragged along.

Don't confuse river otters with **SEA OTTERS**, which are much larger and furrier. They often swim on their backs. They never go into freshwater and seldom come ashore. They even sleep afloat.

Sea otters live along on the Pacific Coast, mostly in British Columbia, Washington, and California. They are rare in Oregon, but their many fans hope they get to be more common.

MINK are about the size of house cats but slimmer. Their fur is darker than that of an otter, except for white spots under the chin, on the throat, and sometimes on the belly. Those that live on the beach eat a lot of crabs and fish and the occasional seabird.

Whether you spy them from a beach, a small boat, or a ferry, **ORCAS** are an unforgettable sight. Three kinds of these black and white dolphins live in Pacific Northwest waters.

- **RESIDENT ORCAS** tend to travel in large groups, called pods, and eat salmon. They spend their summers in sheltered straits and inlets in Alaska, British Columbia, and Washington. Scientists name the pods after letters. For example, the three pods that travel most in the Salish Sea are called J, K, and L. When adult whales grow up, they stay with their mothers. The oldest known resident orca is Granny, or J2, who was 105 in 2016. She travels surrounded by her descendants in the J pod.

- **TRANSIENT ORCAS**, also known as Bigg's orcas, travel in small groups and eat sea mammals such as seals, sea lions, and other whales.

- **OFFSHORE ORCAS** range through the open ocean. Sharks are a big part of their diet.

ROCKWEED, or fucus, a brown seaweed, lives on rocks high up on the beach. It has balloons at the end of its leaves that help the seaweed float upward toward the light when the tide is in. When the tide goes out, the seaweed can get dried to a crisp, but it's still alive and getting energy from the sun.

BULL KELP is a seaweed that grows just offshore. In the springtime this brown seaweed grows fast. Scientists have measured these seaweeds growing two inches in a day. At one end of the kelp a gas-filled float keeps the plant close to the surface and the light. At the other end a rootlike holdfast grips the rock. By June the kelp has grown to form undersea forests, which provide places for sea animals to feed or take shelter.

Some animals live on the kelp itself, at least during the summer. Kelp crabs clamber around on the stalks and blades. Tiny animals called *bryozoans* build colonies that look like white spots on the kelp. Sea slugs called *nudibranchs* roam around and lay their eggs on the kelp. In fall storms sweep the kelp away, and it washes up on the beach in tangled mats.

FRESHWATER

Pick up a river rock. Chances are it is rounded, with no sharp corners. They all were scoured away as the water tumbled the rock downstream. Rivers and creeks also carve channels in the earth as they flow.

The water doesn't move as fast in lakes and ponds, but that doesn't mean they stay the same. They rise and fall with the seasons. Beaver dams make ponds deeper. Dirt carried downstream settles on pond bottoms, making them shallower. And through it all, living things thrive.

It is important to be careful around water. Do not explore any body of water—even a small one—unless an adult says it's OK. Be particularly careful around fast-moving water. It is easy to lose your balance in a river or creek, and the water currents can be powerful.

AMERICAN BEAVER
Castor canadensis

CHUM SALMON
Oncorhynchus keta

MALLARD
Anas platyrhynchos

**BROADLEAF
CATTAILS**
Typha latifolia

**ROCKY MOUNTAIN
POND LILIES**
Nuphar polysepala

**COMMON
DUCKWEED**
Lemna minor

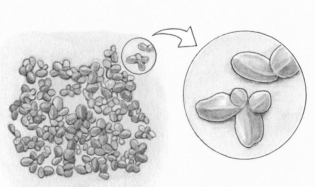

DRAGONFLY
Aeshna

MARSH WREN
Cistothorus palustris

COMMON WATER STRIDER
Aquarius remigis

PACIFIC CHORUS FROG
Pseudacris regilla

RED-WINGED BLACKBIRD
Agelaius phoeniceus

AMERICAN DIPPER
Cinclus mexicanus

COASTAL TAILED FROG
Ascaphus truei

PIED-BILLED GREBE
Podilymbus podiceps

PAINTED TURTLE
Chrysemys picta

Spawning **SALMON** have one mission: to reach the bend in the river where they themselves hatched as eggs, in order to lay or fertilize eggs of their own. They swim like crazy, jumping over waterfalls, fighting through rapids, and snaking through shallows, until they find the right place.

Nothing else matters to them at this stage in their life. They don't eat. A white fungus grows on their skin because their bodies no longer defend against disease. Males' jaws become hooked, and their teeth grow into long spikes for warding off rivals. They also change color, no longer matching the gray and white fish you see in the supermarket. Coho turn red. Sockeye turn red with bright-green heads. Pink salmon turn green, and the males grow humps. Chum turn green with red and brown stripes. Chinook turn brown. Steelhead and cutthroat—which are often called trout, but are actually a kind of salmon—change to have greenish brown backs and red bellies.

Although salmon are born in rivers, they spend years in the ocean, some migrating hundreds—even thousands—of miles. It's amazing that they are able to find their way back to their spawning grounds, where they were born.

Some scientists think that they use the earth's magnetic field to find their way.

Their direction finding isn't perfect, though, while most of them find their way to where they were born, a few end up going to different streams. So when people take away dams, as they did

CHUM SALMON LIFE CYCLE

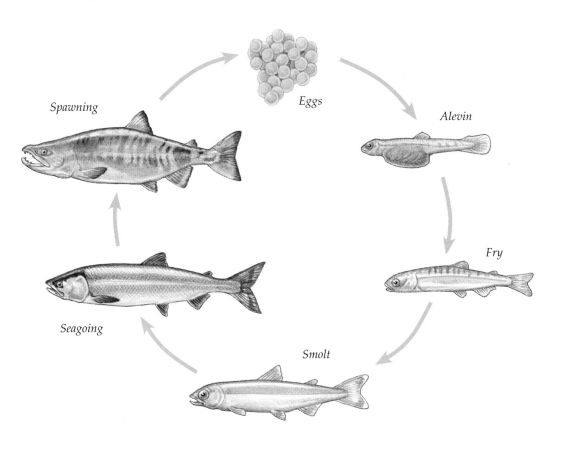

Spawning

Eggs

Alevin

Fry

Smolt

Seagoing

on the Elwha River, salmon will show up and spawn where no salmon have been in generations.

Scientists know a few things about how salmon find the right place to spawn once they are in the river. For one thing, it smells right. Salmon smell using little pits in front of their eyes, and they can smell things along the riverbank. The type of trees overhanging, the rocks in the water, another stream going in—all these change the smell of the water, so fish can remember precisely where to go once they are in the river.

Once salmon have swum, fluttered, and thrashed their way to just the right bend on just the right stream under just the right tree, the female chooses a spot on the pebbly bottom. Then she turns on her side and whacks the rocks with her tail until she makes a hollow in the streambed.

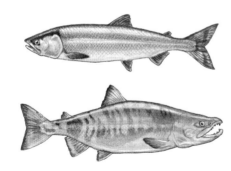

When it is time to spawn, salmon's bodies change color and shape.

When a male comes along, he will stay near her and fight any other male who approaches. When the female finishes digging, she lays hundreds of eggs, and whichever male has won the battle to be closest to the eggs fertilizes them. Then the female sweeps pebbles over the eggs and moves on to build another nest.

Soon after the adults spawn, they die, with the exception of one species: some adult steelhead trout survive spawning, return to the ocean, and come back again for multiple years.

Fish that spend part of their lives in freshwater and part of their lives in salt water are *anadromous*. Some salmon species aren't anadromous. Kokanees are the same species as sockeye salmon, and rainbow trout are the same as steelheads, but kokanees and rainbow trout spend their adult lives in lakes, rather than the ocean.

Here's a way to remember the five main kinds of Pacific salmon using your hand:
Thumb rhymes with chum.
Point your index finger at a friend. Sockeye!
Your middle finger is the biggest, so it's the king, another name for Chinook.
Your ring finger is where you put silver, another name for coho.
Your pinkie stands for pink.

Many animals gather at rivers to eat spawning salmon. Bears eat them. So do eagles. In late fall and winter hundreds, sometimes thousands, of bald eagles gather at rivers with chum salmon runs to eat the carcasses. What the birds and bears don't eat, insects will. The bodies of salmon also fertilize the trees surrounding the river.

Months later, the salmon eggs hatch. The tiny fish that come out—alevins—are still attached to the yolk sac from the egg. At first they hide in the rocks at the bottom of the stream and get their energy from the

yolk. When the yolk sac is gone, they grow into fry and hunt some of the insects that ate the carcasses of their parents.

Different kinds of salmon stay in freshwater for different amounts of time. Sockeyes can spend four years in freshwater, while chum and pink salmon swim to the sea within weeks of losing their egg sac. When they go to sea, they become smolts. They lose the stripes they had as fry, and their tint goes from the brown of the river to the silvery green blue of the ocean. As they get bigger, they range farther away. Then, two to eight years later,

depending on the species, they will return to the river.

BEAVERS can live in streams, rivers, ponds, or lakes. They are hard to spot because they are most active between the evening and the early morning and they tend to dive out of sight when discovered. But if there are beavers around, it is easy to find their work.

Look for these busy-beaver signs:

1. Tree stumps with bite marks: To cut down a tree, a beaver stands at its base and gnaws at it with its strong teeth. The main reason beavers cut down trees is for food. Beavers live through the winter by snacking on the inner bark of trees. They bite the

trunk and branches into pieces, drag them to the water, and tuck them into the mud. The average beaver cuts down two hundred trees a year. Most of the trees are small, but sometimes a couple of beavers will work together to bring down a larger one. When beavers bring a tree down, they don't necessarily kill it. Many of their favorite foods, including cottonwood, willow, and alder, are trees that will often grow new branches after being cut.

Beaver Lodge

2. Lodges: Beavers make dome-shaped homes, or lodges, out of mud and logs. They are big—you might have trouble fitting one into a garage—and strong enough to keep land predators out. The entrances are underwater, so beavers can go in and out unseen. Families of beavers will live at the same lodge year-round for years. Often lodges are in the middle of ponds or on the banks of rivers.

3. Dams: Ponds are useful for beavers. The water barrier keeps predators back, and the mud at the bottom is a good place to store food. The way they make ponds is by building dams. They construct the dams out of boulders, mud, and logs and watch over them carefully, packing on more mud and wood whenever a leak appears.

4. New ponds: When beavers dam a stream, the life of a pond slowly takes it over. Seeds blow in on the wind, or plants could come in on the feet of ducks. Insects lay their eggs, and frogs and salamanders find their way there. Meanwhile, the water flowing into the pond will bring mud called *silt*. After many years, the silt might build up enough to fill the pond entirely.

CATTAILS provide shelter for birds and fish in lakes and ponds. Birds use the fluffy seeds to line their nests. The roots are even edible—like potatoes. Beavers, and sometimes people, dig them up to eat.

POND LILIES need contact with the air, so the tops of their leaves have a waxy surface, which keeps them dry. If you drop some water on the top of a lily pad, you'll notice how it beads and runs off. If you drop water on the bottom of the lily pad, it will spread on the leaf. The leaves, stems, and flowers of pond lilies provide shelter for creatures.

DUCKWEED is the tiniest and simplest of flowering plants: just a leaf with a root dangling in the water. But what it lacks in size, it can make up for in numbers. A single duckweed plant can clone itself again and again, so if nothing is eating it, the duckweed can easily turn the surface of a pond into a green carpet. Luckily lots of things do eat duckweed, including some fish and—yes—ducks. Ducks also help spread the duckweed around—the roots are sticky and easily become entangled in duck feathers or feet, so when the duck flies to the next pond, the duckweed goes too.

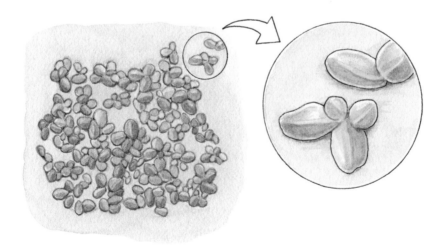

AMERICAN DIPPERS are songbirds, like robins or
sparrows, but unlike robins or sparrows, they live
and feed in fast-running water. They use their strong
toes to grip the rocks of a stream as they search for
insects and other tasty morsels. They can swim, using their wings
to "fly" underwater. They can also fly through waterfalls. The
water beads and rolls off their thick coat of feathers as they bob
in and out of streams, even in the middle of winter.

MALLARDS are the most common duck in the world. The male
has a shiny green head, and the female is brown. Both have
elegant blue patches on their wings. Many winter in the Pacific
Northwest, and they flock on ponds. During fall and winter
males and females form pairs. Sometimes you can see a male
and female together, both nodding their heads—that's part of the
courtship dance.

In the spring females build hidden nests on the ground, lay
eggs, and sit on them for four weeks until the eggs are ready to
hatch. One female can have as many as twelve ducklings. As
soon as the egg goo on their downy feathers dries, ducklings are
able to walk, swim, and catch their own food.

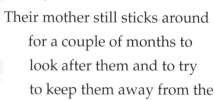

Their mother still sticks around
for a couple of months to
look after them and to try
to keep them away from the

many predators looking for a duckling snack. She usually leaves when they have been able to fly for a week or two.

The male **RED-WINGED BLACKBIRD** is handsome. Most of his body is glossy black. On his shoulders he has patches of red bordered in bright yellow. If he chooses, he can tuck most of the red under his other feathers, but when he's in his territory, he shows off. He's likely to perch at the top of a tall tree or shrub and loudly sing "Conk-la-ree!" while puffing up his shoulders. Sometimes he'll fly over his territory as slowly as possible, flashing his red feathers. He'll chase off other males, and he'll also take on predators such as crows, eagles, and even people. If he's good at keeping intruders away, the females will take notice.

Females' dappled coats of brown and cream feathers make them harder to see, and they don't sing like the male, but if you take a careful look in the bushes around a singing male, you can find them perched around. A good-looking, loud-singing male usually has five or more females nesting around him. Some have as many as fifteen.

PIED-BILLED GREBES build floating nests. Each spring a male and a female will pick a spot to build a nest together. They'll find cattail stems, twigs, or anything that floats and make a bowl-shaped platform that is big enough to hold the weight of several grebes and anchored well enough to stay put on windy days. Then the female will lay the eggs, and both the male and female will take turns incubating the eggs until the chicks are born. They stay together to raise their babies that will sometimes ride around on one of their parents' backs.

It takes some looking to see a MARSH WREN, but it's not hard to hear them as they fly around the cattails. The males know a lot of complicated songs. Scientists have found that these little brown birds can recall and repeat two hundred different combinations of chirps, trills, rattles, whistles, and odd machine noises.

The male marsh wren builds several nests in his territory, anchored to cattails. The nests are oval with an entrance in the side. The outside is made of grasses and other bits of plants. The inside has feathers and soft down. Females will either pick one nest or reject them all and build their own. Successful males will have two or more females nesting in their territory. The nests the females don't choose come in handy when the wrens need to take shelter.

The larvae of many CADDIS FLIES build cases for themselves out of silk, weaving in sticks, leaves, needles, or rocks. The cases are like armor, protecting their soft bodies from predators and from the knocks they might get from sticks and stones carried by water. The cases also help the insects hide. It's very hard to see a caddis fly case when it is next to piles of the rocks or needles that the caddis fly uses to construct its case.

In fast-moving water caddis fly cases are flat and round, like a turtle shell. Caddis flies that live in still water make cases that look like long tubes.

DRAGONFLIES are predators. They catch other insects in midair. Some don't even land to eat. Many mate in the air and fly around attached to one another. Eventually, the female will lay her eggs on a plant, a bit of mud on the bank, or even on the surface of the water so that when the eggs hatch, the larvae will wiggle out into a pond or stream and start eating other bugs.

Before it takes to the air, the dragonfly larva is the fiercest thing in the pond. A big one can eat small fish and tadpoles— anything it can catch. At the bottom of its mouth it has a part called a *labium*, which ends with two wicked hooks. Usually the labium stays tucked away, but when the larva gets close enough to its dinner, the labium will shoot out and hook the prey. It takes less than thirty milliseconds—that is, less than half the time it takes you to blink your eye.

Dragonfly Larva

The tiny **WHIRLIGIG BEETLE** swims around on the surface of the water. An air bubble under its abdomen keeps it afloat. Whirligig beetles have two eyes, each split in two parts. The top half looks up into the air, the bottom looks down into the water. They get their name from the way they move: in fast, energetic circles, like tiny glossy bumper cars.

WATER STRIDERS glide on top of the surface of the water. Their four back legs are covered in hairs that keep the water from reaching their legs, and they slide along without breaking through the surface. It's a little like sliding on the floor of a bouncy house in socks. They eat insects that fall into the water, struggle, and drown. Their two front legs are curled up, ready to grab anything they find as they move along.

TAILED FROGS live in cold, quick-running streams. Their tadpoles cling to rocks using suction cups around their mouths. They eat the algae that cover those rocks. Tailed frogs remain tadpoles for two years or more. When they become adults, they still live in the stream.

These frogs don't have voices, and their ears are incomplete. While most frogs have round eardrums in the skin behind their eyes, tailed frogs don't, and they don't hear at all.

Some people think this may be because they live in loud places. The rushing water is so loud that they wouldn't be able to hear a predator approaching, a mate calling, or any of the other things that animals usually use hearing for. They are better off relying on their senses of sight, smell, and touch.

When **PACIFIC CHORUS FROGS** first come out of the pond to start hunting on land, they are small enough to perch on a dime. At their biggest they're only two inches long. But at night they can fill the air with noise. When the males call for the females in the spring, their "ribbit, ribbit, ribbit" can measure ninety decibels—about as loud as a bulldozer engine.

On a floating log in a pond, you can sometimes see rows of **TURTLES** soaking up the sun. The turtles are in ponds year-round, though during the coldest months, they stay still in the mud at the bottom. At the end of summer the female digs a hole in a sunny spot near the pond and lays her eggs. They hatch in the fall but sometimes don't come out of the nest until the spring. Then the baby turtles crawl down to the pond.

BACKYARDS AND URBAN PARKS

You don't have to go to the wilderness to experience nature. There are many interesting wild animals and plants that thrive in your backyard, your neighborhood, and urban parks. You just need to know where to look.

The first step in finding nature in your neighborhood is to spend time outside. Walk to school and other places you need to go. Explore parks. If you have to wait outside somewhere, say, a bus stop, don't always pass the time with an electronic device. Look around and see what living things thrive among the buildings and concrete.

RACCOON
Procyon lotor

EASTERN GRAY SQUIRREL
Sciurus carolinensis

HUMMINGBIRD
Calypte anna

BUSHTIT
Psaltriparus minimus

AMERICAN CROW
Corvus brachyrhynchos

NORTHERN FLICKER
Colaptes auratus

ROBIN
Turdus migratorius

**CABBAGE WHITE
BUTTERFLY**
Pieris rapae

BUMBLEBEE
Bombus

PAVEMENT ANT
*Tetramorium
caespitum*

YELLOW JACKET
Vespula

EUROPEAN EARWIG
Forficula auricularia

HOVERFLY
Syrphidae

LADYBUG
Harmonia axyridis

CROSS ORB WEAVER SPIDER
Araneus diadematus

PILL BUG
Armadillidium vulgare

RACCOONS roam around yards and alleyways in urban areas. Like us, they are *omnivores*, meaning they eat both plants and animals, and they're smart enough to figure out how to find food in many places. For example, along with fishing crabs off the beach, they'll help themselves to dog food or garbage.

They usually hunt and move around at night, and rest during the day in hollow trees, rock piles, or even crawl spaces or under people's decks. The only time they stay in one place is when a mother gives birth to babies, called kits.

The kits are born tiny—about the size of a bar of soap. Their eyes are closed, and they have no teeth. It takes eight weeks for them to grow big and strong enough to leave their den, but even then their mother carries them around sometimes. They stay in the same territory as their mother for thirteen months or more. She protects them and shows them how to find food and climb trees. As they grow older, they become more independent and go out more on their own.

EASTERN GRAY SQUIRRELS run, climb, feed, and squabble during the daytime, though they are most active around sunrise and sunset. They build big ball-shaped nests in trees and snuggle up in them on cold winter days. They are not native to the Pacific Northwest.

The **ROBIN** is one of the first birds to sing in the morning and the last to sing at night. The male robin sings to attract females and announce his territory to other males. The female makes a cup-shaped nest out of mud, twigs, grass, and other things she finds, such as pieces of paper or ribbons. Usually robins will nest in a tree or a bush, but they have also been known to nest on the rung of a ladder, in a mailbox, or atop a street sign.

The female lays three or four eggs and sits on them for about twelve days while the male stands guard. When the eggs hatch, both parents work hard to feed the chicks and keep the nest clean.

Robins can have three sets of chicks a year, but most of the chicks don't live long enough to learn to fly. Predators such as raccoons or crows often eat the eggs or chicks.

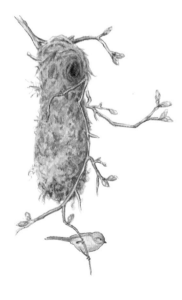

Male and female **BUSHTITS** work together to weave a nest out of moss, spiderwebs, grasses, and bits of plants. The nest dangles from a tree branch, looking like an old fuzzy green sock. The entrance is at the top, and the babies nestle in the warm place at the bottom. Looking after the nest is hard work. In spring and summer adult bushtits with nests often have bent or ragged tail feathers.

HUMMINGBIRDS' wings beat so fast that they are difficult to see, and while they are flying, their hearts can beat more than twenty times per second. They drink nectar from flowers (and hummingbird feeders), using their long tongues, which extend out beyond their long beaks. They also snack on tiny insects, catching them from the air, collecting them from leaves, or even plucking them out of spiderwebs.

While they are amazing fliers, they are terrible walkers. Their feet aren't good for much other than gripping branches. If they need to change position on a branch, they fly down the branch.

Hummingbirds—especially male hummingbirds—compete fiercely over feeders or patches of flowers. It's fun to watch them zoom after each other.

You would be very lucky to find a hummingbird nest. The female bird uses spiderwebs to stick lichen and bark on the nest so that it's camouflaged to look like part of a tree branch.

NORTHERN FLICKERS nest in holes in trees, telephone poles, or buildings, whatever comes in handy. In the spring the males like to drum on wood, siding on buildings, or metal chimneys—the louder the better. When they are not nesting, drumming, or visiting bird feeders, these birds with polka-dot bellies often hop along the ground, looking for ants and beetles.

If you see one CROW, keep looking. There will be at least one more nearby. Crows have strong family bonds. In the winter they often feed in large groups. Pairs of crows keep nesting together year after year. In the spring when a pair of crows nests, often one of their sons from the year before will help them build a nest and feed the young.

Crows usually construct their nests by interweaving twigs and lining them with soft stuff such as grasses, but they will use whatever they can find. Crows have been known to build nests out of coat hangers or pieces of plastic.

When young crows start to leave the nest, typically around May, adult crows can become very aggressive toward people and dogs, diving and pecking at them if they get too close to their nests and babies. Give them some space. This season will be done soon.

In the winter crows fly away to sleep, or roost, at night on the edge of the city. At sunset you can sometimes see lines of hundreds of crows heading for the roost. At sunrise you can see them coming back.

BARN SWALLOW males and females work together to build a nest out of mud and straw, somewhere under a roof. They like barns, baseball dugouts, bridges, and eaves. They are amazing fliers. They eat by catching insects midair. If you watch a group of swallows in summer sometimes you can see one pass an insect to another while both are flying. It's most likely an adult feeding a young one just ready to hunt. Both parents help feed (and pick up poop blobs from) the baby swallows, and sometimes other adults help too.

ORB WEAVER SPIDERS make a web that looks like a spiral with spokes. They can't see well, but they can sense very clearly with their legs. Different hairs on their legs help them taste, track air currents, sense vibrations, and smell.

How do they keep from getting caught in their own webs? By walking very carefully. Orb weaver spiders step around the sticky parts of their webs and have oil and special claws on the ends of their feet to grip the threads.

FLOWER SPIDERS hunt by hiding in flowers—they can change color from yellow to white—and pouncing on bees or butterflies that come looking for the flower's nectar. Their poison can stop a bee several times their size. If you look at a flower and see a bee or a butterfly that's totally still, there may be a flower spider about.

HONEYBEES live in large colonies. Humans take care of many of them, but there are also wild honeybees taking refuge in hollow trees and other hideaways. Each colony has one queen and a few hundred male drones. The remaining bees are female worker bees, such as the ones you see foraging from flower to flower. On a single trip from the hive, a worker bee visits more than fifty flowers. On a good day, she can visit two thousand.

BUMBLEBEES are like honeybees, except that their bodies are bigger and their hives are smaller. The queen bee wakes in early spring, gathers nectar and pollen, builds some wax cells in a space such as a woodpecker hole or mouse hole, and then raises a brood of larvae. She nestles her furry body next to her babies, then vibrates her flight muscles continuously until her body reaches the best temperature for her larvae. If the temperature goes down, she vibrates her muscles again. When the larvae are big enough, they can gather food and take care of the queen as she has more larvae.

Don't let the yellow stripes of the **HOVERFLY** fool you. This insect can't sting you at all. It's not a bee or wasp. Its colors tell predators to leave it alone. It drinks nectar and carries pollen from flower to flower, just like a bee. Unlike a bee's larvae, hoverfly maggots eat aphids. And the hoverfly can hover. It looks like it is hanging still next to the flower.

YELLOW JACKETS are not the same as bees. When a honeybee stings you, its stinger becomes lodged in your skin and the bee dies. A yellow jacket wasp can sting you, pull its stinger out, and sting you again. Because of this, yellow jackets are more likely to sting than honeybees.

Yellow jackets build nests out of paper. They chew wood, and the combination of chewed wood and wasp spit makes paper,

Keep a close watch on the flowers in your yard, and you'll see a huge variety of other creatures seeking sweetness in flowers. There are mason bees, which are fuzzy blue bees, about the same size as honeybees, that fly in the spring. Later in the summer you might see sweat bees, which are tiny and come in brilliant shiny blue and green colors. There are also leaf-cutter bees, which are mostly black with narrow light-colored stripes on their abdomens and hairy bellies that pick up pollen. They bite neat circular pieces out of leaves and petals and fly away with them to line their nests.

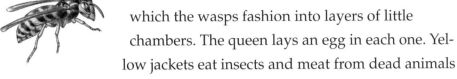

which the wasps fashion into layers of little chambers. The queen lays an egg in each one. Yellow jackets eat insects and meat from dead animals and birds, but they also like to snack on nectar, and when they do, they help pollinate flowers.

BUTTERFLIES are tougher than you might think. For example, they are able to survive the storms and ice of winter. Some of them, such as painted ladies, admirals, and monarchs, do it by migrating hundreds of miles—not bad for a creature that might weigh less than a paper clip.

Others stay put, surviving as eggs or as *pupae* (the stage in which a caterpillar rests inside a case called a *chrysalis*, turning into an adult). A few winter as adults.

During the first spring days, when it is warm enough for you to go out without a sweater, it is finally warm enough for butterflies to fly, and the ones that hid through the winter as adults will be the very first to appear. Their wings are bright on top, but underneath, they are the color of dead leaves. Soon afterward you'll see the cabbage white, a very common white butterfly that spends the winter as a pupa.

These butterflies are named cabbage whites because as caterpillars they eat plants from the mustard family, which includes cabbage, kale, broccoli, brussels sprouts, and other plants people would rather not share with caterpillars. After mating the female lays eggs on the underside of a leaf of a plant from the mustard family. When the pale-green caterpillars hatch, they settle in to eat.

If you want to tell a male EUROPEAN EARWIG from a female, take a look at the pincers on its abdomen. Males have curved pincers, while females have straighter pincers. Earwigs have wings, though the wings are very hard to see. They use their pincers like tweezers to help unfold their wings, defend their nests, and sometimes catch prey.

Earwigs hide during the day, but you can come across them if you look in shady, moist places, such as under a piece of loose bark.

The females are good mothers. They dig underground burrows and take care of their eggs, cleaning them and rearranging them until they are ready to hatch.

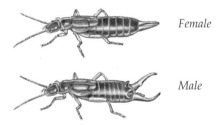

Female

Male

MOSQUITOES can beat their wings six hundred times per second. Only the female mosquito is interested in your blood. She needs one good blood meal to feed her eggs. Male mosquitoes don't bite and have big feathery antennae, which they use to listen for females. If you want to see if you can attract male mosquitoes (which don't bite), try imitating the high note that female mosquitoes make when flying.

There are more than four hundred kinds of LADYBUGS in North America. Most of them are red or orange beetles with black spots, and gardeners prize their ability to eat aphids and insect eggs. Ladybugs spend the winter in a sheltered place and then come out in early spring. Adults lay oval yellow eggs under a leaf where aphids are likely to be plentiful. From the eggs hatch mostly black spiky larvae that eat until it's time for them to transform into adults. Then they attach to a sheltered spot, such as the back of a leaf or the shady side of a house, and stay still. After a few days, they will break out of their old larval exoskeletons as fully formed adult ladybugs.

Ladybug Larva

PILL BUGS are little gray animals that have fourteen legs, two pairs of antennae, and seven plates on their back, which fit so that if the animal is threatened, it can curl up into a little ball the size of a pea.

They go by a lot of names. People from Washington or Oregon call them potato bugs or roly-polies. Many British Columbians call them wood lice. A few people call them doodlebugs.

Whatever you call them, pill bugs are interesting creatures. They are *isopods*, a kind of crustacean, not insects. The females carry their eggs in a pouch, and after the eggs hatch, they carry their young around until the little ones are ready to stand on their own fourteen feet and forage for their own food. Even then, they tend to stay close to their mother. If you see a big pill bug surrounded by little ones, it's probably a mother and her babies.

EARTHWORMS eat dirt as they move underground through the soil. They grind it up, digest food from it, and then poop it out as they go. If it rains hard, they'll come to the surface. Scientists think they do this because they can move faster on the surface than they can underground. Normally they'd dry out on the surface, but the heavy rain keeps them moist.

Another creature that will come out in the rain is a SNAIL. When it is dry, they take refuge under rocks and logs and sometimes seal themselves in their shells, but when it rains, they go on the move in search of food and mates.

PAVEMENT ANTS are so small that one could hide behind a grain of rice, and they build their nests underground, often under sidewalks, so most of the time we don't notice them. But on warm days in spring they come out in the open by the thousands. Armies of them from different nests will confront each other for a piece of sidewalk crack. From a human's-eye view, it looks like a piece of brown velvet on the sidewalk. From an ant's-eye view, it's war, as groups of ants grab each other and try to tear each other apart.

Pavement ants come above ground on warm days and fight for territory.

NATURE YEAR-ROUND IN THE PACIFIC NORTHWEST

Every time you look at the world outside, something has changed. Here is a list of some of the events that happen in the natural world over the course of a year. Depending on where you live in the Pacific Northwest, the timing might be different. For example, if you are in British Columbia, spring will come later and fall will come earlier than if you live in Oregon.

Winter

- Highest tide of the year occurs.

- Bucks, or male deer, begin to lose their antlers.

- As they set up their territories, barred and great horned owls can become aggressive, swooping down on unwary joggers and walkers in parks and other wooded areas.

- Great horned owls take over old nests made by other birds (such as crows or hawks) and lay eggs.

- Pacific chorus frogs start calling on warm nights. If the temperature drops below forty-one degrees Fahrenheit, they stop.

- First bumblebees emerge.

- Male robins sing.

- Great blue herons begin building nests.

Spring

- Family groups of crows stop going to night roosts and spend their days in their breeding territories. Usually the family group is a male, a female, and sometimes a helper, which is often one of their male offspring from the year before. Many immature crows keep using the night roosts.

- Northern flickers start drumming.

- Spring is mating season for rough-skinned newts. They migrate through the forest to ponds and lakes and lay their eggs in the water.

- After spending the winter roaming the Pacific Coast, resident orcas return to the Salish Sea.

- First dragonflies, including green darners (green and blue dragonflies), migrate north from California and other warm places.

- First butterflies fly. Some, such as cabbage whites, will have newly emerged from cocoons. Others will have hibernated through the winter as adults.

- Ospreys arrive from Mexico and Central America.

- Barn swallows arrive from Central and South America.

- Baby crows leave the nest and start exploring, with adults nearby ready to dive on anything or anyone that looks threatening.

- Buffleheads leave coastal waters for their breeding grounds in aspen forests by ponds and lakes in Canada and Alaska.

- Plankton reaches its peak in the Salish Sea.

- Fawns are born.

Summary

Summer

- Harbor seals are born.

- Many jellies can be found in sea water.

- Young great blue herons leave nests.

- Plankton begins to decline in the Salish Sea.

- Winged male and female Pacific dampwood termites crawl out of their colonies and take flight on warmer evenings.

- Green darners, the offspring of those that arrived from the south in spring, emerge from ponds and head south for the winter.

- Barn swallows fly south for the winter.

- Although there are just as many spiders around as usual, their webs are bigger so people notice them more.

- Ospreys fly south for the winter.

Fall

- Licorice ferns turn green and grow after resting dormant through the summer.

- Buffleheads arrive from inland lakes for the winter, along with many other water birds.

- A few days after fall rains come, mushrooms appear on the forest floor.

- Snow begins to fall in the mountains.

- Storms pull kelp loose, and leave it tangled on the beach.

- All crows leave the cities every night to fly to their winter roosts, banding together in groups of ten thousand or more for warmth and protection. In the morning they fly back to their feeding areas.

- Mating season begins for deer.

- The last dragonflies of the year, brilliant reddish autumn meadowhawks, make their last flights before the first heavy frosts in October or November. They are able to keep going late in the year because they spend a lot of time basking in the sun.

- Chum salmon spawn.

- Eagles gather on rivers and eat salmon that have died after spawning.

- Resident orcas often leave local waters to forage along ocean coasts.

INDEX

FIONA COHEN is a science writer whose work has appeared in the *Seattle Post-Intelligencer*, *Georgia Straight*, *Times Colonist*, and *Canadian Geographic*. She grew up investigating tide pools on the beaches of Victoria, BC, and now lives in Seattle.

MARNI FYLLING is a science illustrator, author, and educator who loves tide pooling, hiking, and sketching outside. Her most recent book is *Fylling's Illustrated Guide to Pacific Coast Tide Pools*.